# Head, Shoulders, Knees, and Toes

# For Olivia

ISBN 978-0-545-15604-2

Text copyright © 2009 by Scholastic Inc.
Illustrations copyright © 2009 by Mike Wohnoutka.
All rights reserved. Published by Scholastic Inc.
SCHOLASTIC, SING AND READ STORYBOOK, and associated logos
are trademarks and/or registered trademarks of Scholastic Inc.

13 12 11 10 9 8 7 6 5                    10 11 12 13 14 15/0
                                                          40
Printed in the U.S.A.
First printing, September 2009

Book design by Jennifer Rinaldi Windau

# Head, Shoulders, Knees, and Toes

Illustrated by
Mike Wohnoutka

Scholastic Inc.
New York Toronto London Auckland
Sydney Mexico City New Delhi Hong Kong

Head, shoulders, knees, and toes.

Head, shoulders, knees, and toes.

Eyes . . .

and ears ...

...and mouth

and nose.

Head, shoulders, knees, and toes.

Head, shoulders, knees, and toes.

Head, shoulders, knees, and toes.

Eyes ...

...and mouth and nose.

Head, shoulders, knees, and toes.

# Head, Shoulders, Knees, and Toes

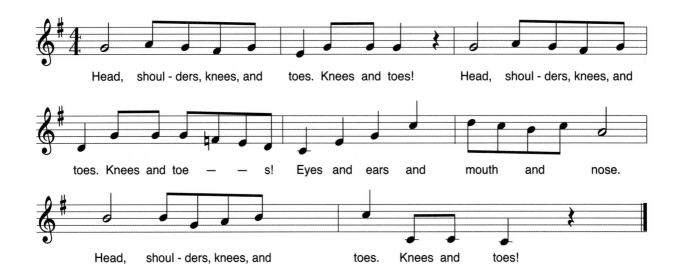

Head, shoul - ders, knees, and toes. Knees and toes! Head, shoul - ders, knees, and

toes. Knees and toe — — s! Eyes and ears and mouth and nose.

Head, shoul - ders, knees, and toes. Knees and toes!